CONTENTS

A Star Emerges

Troy Aikman couldn't believe his eyes. This is too good to be true, thought the Dallas Cowboys' young quarterback. This is a sure thing.

It was the second quarter of Super Bowl XXVII on January 31, 1993. Aikman's club had a narrow 14–10 lead over the Buffalo Bills. The Cowboys had the ball deep in Bills territory. Aikman called a play that would let running back Emmitt Smith plow through the Buffalo defensive line.

But as Aikman set to take the snap from center, he noticed that the Buffalo defenders were ignoring Michael Irvin, his favorite receiver. Yes, Aikman thought, this is too good to be true. This is a sure thing.

TROY AIKMAN

Hall of Fame Football Superstar

Glen
Macnow

Library of Congress Cataloging-in-Publication Data
Macnow, Glen.
  Troy Aikman : hall of fame football superstar / Glen Macnow.
    pages cm. — (Hall of fame sports greats)
  Includes bibliographical references and index.
  Summary: "Learn about Hall of Fame quarterback Troy Aikman in this sports biography. See how he went from a small town star in Oklahoma to a three-time Super Bowl winning champion with the Dallas Cowboys"—Provided by publisher.
  ISBN 978-1-62285-040-2
  1. Aikman, Troy, 1966- —Juvenile literature. 2. Football players—United States—Biography—Juvenile literature. 3. Dallas Cowboys (Football team)—Juvenile literature. I. Title.
  GV939.A46M336 2013
  796.332092—dc23
  [B]
                        2013005596

Paperback ISBN: 978-1-62285-041-9   EPUB ISBN: 978-1-62285-043-3
Single-User PDF ISBN: 978-1-62285-044-0   Multi-User PDF ISBN: 978-1-62285-151-5

Printed in the United States of America

052013 Lake Book Manufacturing, Inc., Melrose Park, IL

10 9 8 7 6 5 4 3 2 1

To Our Readers: We have done our best to make sure all Internet addresses in this book were active and appropriate when we went to press. However, the author and the Publisher have no control over, and assume no liability for, the material available on those Internet sites or on other Web sites they may link to. Any comments or suggestions can be sent by e-mail to comments@speedingstar.com or to the following address:

Speeding Star
Box 398, 40 Industrial Road
Berkeley Heights, NJ 07922
USA
www.speedingstar.com

Photo Credits: AP Images/Charles Krupa, p. 54; AP Images/David Longstreath, p. 44; AP Images/Denis Poroy, p. 16; AP Images/George Widman, p. 36; AP Images/Gret Trott, p. 48; AP Images/Lou Krasky, p. 19; AP Images/Marc Serota, p. 28; AP Images/Mark Duncan, p. 60; AP Images/NFL Photos, pp. 11, 46, 57; AP Images/Ray Stubblebine, p. 26; AP Images/Rob Schumacher, p. 32; AP Images/Ron Heflin, pp. 23, 31, 40; AP Images/Susan Ragan, p. 5; AP Images/Tom DiPace, pp. 1, 8.

Cover Photo: AP Images/Tom DiPace

This book was originally published as *Sports Great Troy Aikman* in 1995.

Thinking fast, he barked out signals to change the play. When he got the ball, Aikman faked a handoff to Smith. The Bills all went for the fake. Then Aikman dropped back a few steps. He lofted a perfect spiral to Irvin, who stood alone in the end zone. Touchdown! Dallas' slim lead suddenly became 11 points. The romp was on.

Two quarters later, the Cowboys strutted off the field with a 52–17 win and the Lombardi Trophy. The game was one of the most one-sided wins in Super Bowl history. Many players could take credit. Like Smith, who rushed for 108 yards and a touchdown. Or Irvin, who caught 6 passes and outran Buffalo's secondary for 114 yards. Or Dallas' entire defense, for having forced the Bills into 8 fumbles and 4 interceptions.

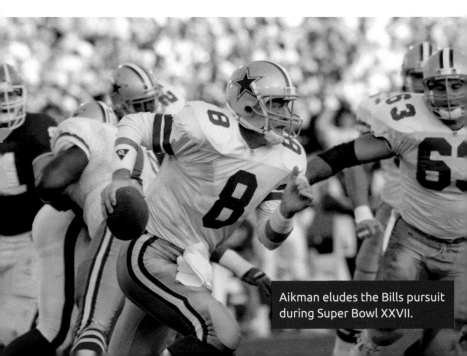

Aikman eludes the Bills pursuit during Super Bowl XXVII.

The biggest hero of all was Aikman. He completed 22 of 30 passes for 273 yards and 4 touchdowns. He was inspirational in calling the plays and directing his teammates. He was everyone's choice for Super Bowl Most Valuable Player (MVP).

In the locker room afterward, Aikman was presented with his MVP trophy and the keys to a luxury car. Reporters gathered around, perhaps expecting him to brag. But that has never been Aikman's style.

"I'm a little bashful receiving this because we have so many great players," Aikman said. "It really is a shame they have to pick one guy."

Well, that's football, Troy. Whether it's fair or not, the quarterback gets most of the glory when his team wins a National Football League (NFL) title. However, when the team loses, as the Cowboys did during Aikman's early years, the quarterback takes most of the heat.

When the team wins, the quarterback gets the biggest applause and the shiniest trophies. So when the Cowboys won the Super Bowl in 1993, and again in 1994, Troy Aikman, a quiet, shy guy from Oklahoma, suddenly emerged as an American hero.

With his powerful body and wholesome good looks, Aikman appeared to be the perfect guy to play the role. During his playing days, he stood 6-feet 4-inches tall and weighed 220 pounds. That was big enough to bang heads with linebackers and still live to talk about it. His pinpoint accurate arm could hit a speedy receiver on the numbers from fifty yards away. His mind was so quick at reading defenses that Cowboys teammates nicknamed him Computer Head.

Those are the ingredients that go into this recipe. The final product is that Aikman led his team to two Super Bowl wins by the age of twenty-seven. Just two quarterbacks have accomplished the feat quicker: Tom Brady of the New England Patriots, and Ben Roethlisberger of the Pittsburg Steelers. Both won their first Super Bowl after Aikman retired.

Indeed, Aikman seemed so perfect at what he did that you almost expected him to have a huge ego. But that's just not him. Fans liked to call Joe Montana magical with his late comebacks, to call Steve Young clever and elusive, or to rave about Jim Kelly's guts. But when people talk about Aikman, they usually just say, "Oh, nice guy." There's nothing cocky or phony about this football star.

"If you were to meet Troy, you'd never think he's a two-time Super Bowl star and the star quarterback for America's Team," said former teammate Nate Newton. "He walks around like he's the guy who works on your car, or teaches your kids, or maybe just lives next door. He's just a regular person."

Just a regular person? Okay, maybe one with a golden arm, a quick mind, and the cool nerves of a brain surgeon. No game showed his ability to stay calm more than that first Super Bowl win over the Bills. It came before 98,374 people at the Rose Bowl in Pasadena, California.

Although he ended up as MVP of that contest, Aikman got off to a rocky start. He completed just three of his first six passes. The Cowboys punted on their first two possessions. Some fans

Even after a big play, Aikman never overly celebrated his accomplishments.

and announcers began to wonder whether Aikman was off that day. But Troy knew things would work out. In fact, he told his teammates, "Don't worry. I feel great today. We're going to win big."

The touchdown pass to Irvin opened the gates that afternoon. But it was only one of many highlights. Aikman also threw a twenty-three-yard TD to tight end Jay Novacek, after fooling the Bills by faking another pass to Irvin. He again connected with the slippery Irvin on an eighteen-yarder in the second quarter. And he showed off his arm strength in the fourth quarter, heaving a forty-five-yard touchdown bullet to wide receiver Alvin Harper. After the game, Harper described it as the most perfect pass he had ever caught.

Two days after the Super Bowl win, the city of Dallas held a big parade for its champions. More than five hundred thousand fans gathered downtown to hear speeches by coaches and players. The one they most wanted to hear was Aikman. He was bashful in front of the big crowd and too embarrassed to talk. Teammates had to pull him to the microphone. When he finally spoke, Aikman said, "No matter what happens in my career from here on out, at least I can say that I took a team to the Super Bowl. And we were able to win it. I guess there aren't a lot of people who get the chance to say something like that."

Throughout his life, Aikman has been proving himself the best at nearly everything he has tried. Folks who remember him growing up back in Henryetta, Oklahoma, say that he could throw a strike to a teammate forty yards away at the age of twelve. In junior high, he couldn't find any receivers courageous enough to catch his bullet passes. While other fourteen year olds were dreaming about playing for their high school team, Aikman was doing it.

He was good enough as a teenage athlete to be offered the chance to play two sports. The New York Mets almost drafted him in baseball, and more than twenty colleges wanted him to play football. Young Troy finally signed as a quarterback close to home at the University of Oklahoma. But he got injured there and ended up sitting on the bench. Eventually, he switched to UCLA. In two years, he led the Bruins to a 20–4 record. As a senior in 1988, he was a finalist for the Heisman Trophy, which goes to the best college football player in the entire country.

That same year, Dallas finished with the worst record in pro football. The terrible season got the Cowboys coach fired. It also gave them the first choice in the 1989 draft of college seniors. When it came time to make the pick, there was little question whom Dallas would select.

"Troy has the talent to take the Cowboys back to where we all want them to be," new coach Jimmy Johnson said on Draft Day. "You would be amazed at what some of the teams were willing to give up in a trade for Troy. But we've known that this was our guy."

In Aikman's first year, things didn't go exactly as he or the coach had planned. The Cowboys had more than a dozen other rookies, including most of the men who blocked for the quarterback. They all suffered through growing pains. No one suffered more than Troy, who was decked so many times that he earned the nickname Timex. That comes from the watch

Aikman celebrates with Emmitt Smith (No. 22) and Michael Irvin (No. 88) after Irvin's touchdown catch during Super Bowl XXVII.

company's old ad slogan, "It takes a licking, but keeps on ticking."

The Cowboys won just one game that season and just seven in 1990. But by 1991, Aikman emerged as a star. The Cowboys made the playoffs that season for the first time in six years. With a young team and a young quarterback, Dallas began to earn respect around the league. Some experts, including then Chicago Bears coach Mike Ditka, predicted that Aikman would lead the Cowboys to a Super Bowl in two or three more years.

Ditka was wrong. It didn't take the Cowboys two or three years to make it. It took just one. In the magical 1992 season, Dallas won 13 regular-season games and lost just three. Aikman, with good players now surrounding him, threw for 23 touchdowns. He made the NFL's all-star game, the Pro Bowl, for the first time.

His shining moment, of course, came in the Super Bowl. Afterward, Aikman would say that his favorite highlight was the first touchdown pass to Irvin, the one that broke open the game.

"When I saw how the Bills weren't covering Michael tight, I could hardly believe my eyes," he said. "It was a very special moment for me, because that's when I realized that we were going to be the champions. It was a long road. It took a lot of different courses to get to where I am now."

Chapter 2

Showing His Talent

As a young boy, Troy Aikman dreamed of becoming a major-league baseball pitcher. Growing up in Cerritos, California, his heroes were players on the Los Angeles Dodgers, not the Los Angeles Rams. Young Troy's arm, a rifle even back then, made him a nine-year-old pitching star in Little League. Football? That was just a game to play on the rare days that it got too chilly for baseball.

That all changed when Troy was twelve. His father, Ken Aikman, got a good job working on an oil pipeline and moved the family to a ranch in tiny Henryetta, Oklahoma. The new neighborhood did not have shopping malls or fast-food restaurants for Troy to bike to. The closest neighbors lived nearly a mile away. Troy was so unhappy about leaving his California friends that he didn't speak to his parents for two weeks. When he finally stopped sulking and looked around his new hometown, he noticed that the kids didn't play baseball nearly as much as football.

Troy had not liked football much since he broke his wrist playing it at age ten. But he wanted to make new friends, and he wanted to please his dad who was a big fan of the sport. So the new eighth-grader went out for football. "In Oklahoma," Troy later explained, "everybody plays football whether they want to or not. It's the manly thing to do."

On the first day of practice in junior high school, the coaches asked Troy to pick a position. He chose quarterback. They handed him a ball. He threw a perfect thirty-yard spiral that stung the hands of the boy who tried to grab it. He threw more passes, but they were too fast for the other kids to catch. So the coaches quickly sent Troy to another field to work out with the older high school boys.

The high school coach, Barry Holt, immediately noticed something funny about the youngster's passing style. Instead of putting all of his fingers on the football's laces, as most quarterbacks do, Troy put only his pinkie on the laces. It was a strange delivery, but it worked for Troy. So the coach wisely decided not to change it. Aikman was the only quarterback in the NFL to handle the ball in this unusual way.

By the time he was fourteen, Troy was starting for the Henryetta High Fighting Hens. The team lost more games than it won in two of Troy's three seasons there, but he became famous around Oklahoma as a strong-armed kid who might someday end up in the NFL. The players and coaches all knew Aikman was special. Local football fans in Henryetta still talk about some of his more memorable plays.

Against Hartshorne High one Friday night, Henryetta was 7 points down in the last 2 minutes. Aikman was trying to drive the Hens to the winning score. He dropped back to pass but was hit by two defensive linemen. As he was falling backward, Aikman reached out and threw a twenty-five-yard sidearm touchdown pass. After the game, Hartshorne's coach told Troy, "We'll be watching you someday on *Monday Night Football*."

Another time, the Fighting Hens were tied with Checotah High, 6–6, with 30 seconds left. Troy threw a seventy-yard touchdown pass to win the game. As his teammates danced and screamed on the sidelines, Troy calmly walked over and drank a glass of water. John Walker, who was a friend and teammate, later said that kind of calm reaction was typical. Aikman never said a lot, Walker explained. A player of his great ability didn't need to say much.

According to Aikman, that's just what he learned from his parents, Ken and Charlyn Aikman. "What I am is a direct result of how I was raised," he said. "I don't understand why guys want to be controversial and in the press all the time. It's just not my nature."

The folks in Henryetta appreciated Troy's modest and friendly ways. Indeed, they still do. The town of 7,000 now has an "Aikman Avenue" and "Home of Troy Aikman" signs on the city limits. After his Super Bowl win, Aikman donated money to help build a children's center in town. He also sponsors a scholarship for students who want to attend college but can't afford to.

That wasn't on his mind back in high school. Back then, he was still trying to make the tough choice between baseball and football. Although he was the state of Oklahoma's top high school quarterback as a senior, Troy still loved playing baseball. He had grown to six-feet-four and was Henryetta High's star catcher and shortstop. The night before Major League Baseball's 1984 Draft of prospects, a scout from the New York Mets came to visit. The scout told Troy that the club was thinking of taking him—as long as his signing-bonus request was reasonable.

The idea was tempting, Troy thought, but it was also wrong. He had promised his father that he would go to college and study to be a doctor. Playing football would earn him

Aikman throws out the ceremonial first pitch at a San Diego Padres game against the Houston Astros. Troy might have been a major-league pitcher if he had taken the New York Mets offer.

that chance to go to college. So Troy blurted out a contract demand, $200,000, that he hoped would be too high for the Mets. The scout's response: "Good luck playing football."

Dozens of college coaches lined up to get Troy. His first choice was Oklahoma State University. The coach there was Jimmy Johnson, who ran a high-octane passing attack that Aikman loved. Years later, Johnson and Aikman would come together as coach and quarterback of the Dallas Cowboys. But back in 1984, Troy was talked out of going to Oklahoma State by Barry Switzer. He was the coach of the University of Oklahoma Sooners.

Switzer was the famous coach at the state's top football program. Every high school player in Oklahoma dreamed of playing for him. Aikman shared that dream. But he was not excited about Switzer's "wishbone" offense. It used the quarterback more as a runner than as a passer. Aikman had a golden arm and wanted to use it.

"No problem," Switzer said. Because Aikman was so talented, the coach told him, the school would change its offensive plan. With Aikman as quarterback, Switzer promised to drop the wishbone for a wide-open passing game.

Troy believed the promise. He signed up for the school. Later he learned that Switzer had told other people he would never change his offensive plan for anyone. "I guess I got suckered," Aikman said. "Coach Switzer talked to me about playing for the Orange Bowl and the national championship every year. I wanted to do those things."

Stuck in a bad situation, Troy decided to make the best of

it. He outworked his teammates, on the field and off. He always carried a notepad, writing down every word said by every coach. When no one else knew the answer, recalled offensive coordinator Tony Brown, coaches could ask Troy. He would always know it. Aikman was driven to be a great player.

As an eighteen-year-old freshman, Troy was forced into a starting role against Kansas when quarterback Danny Bradley was injured. As hard as he had worked, he wasn't ready. He completed just 2 of 14 pass attempts for 8 yards and 3 interceptions. The Sooners lost, 28–11. Some of the hometown fans booed Aikman.

The next season, 1985, Troy was more prepared. He started Oklahoma's first three games, all wins. Coach Switzer, impressed with Aikman's arm, was letting him throw more passes. In the fourth game, against the University of Miami, Aikman completed 6 of 7 passes for 131 yards and a touchdown in the first quarter. Oklahoma seemed ready to win the game. Then disaster struck.

Aikman dropped back to pass early in the second quarter. Miami blitzed, meaning it sent six pass rushers after the quarterback. Two of them caught Aikman, rolled over him and broke his ankle. His season was finished.

So was his career as a Sooner. Freshman Jamelle Holieway took over the quarterback's job. He led Oklahoma to a national championship. When the next season started, Holieway had the job. Troy was back on the bench. "We will see Aikman in the NFL," Coach Switzer said at the time. "We will not see Jamelle Holieway in the NFL. But Holieway fits our system

Troy transferred to UCLA prior to the 1986 season. He was excited to go back to Southern California for the first time since he was a child.

better." (Holieway ended up playing two years in the NFL for the Raiders.)

Aikman knew that to get to the NFL, he'd have to first be a star at another college. So he went to see Switzer. The coach offered to help by calling coaches he knew to see who might be interested in a rifle-armed quarterback coming off an ankle injury.

One of Switzer's first calls went to Terry Donahue, head coach at the University of California at Los Angeles. Donahue didn't know much about Troy. Switzer promised him that Troy was better than any other quarterback UCLA had. That was good enough for Donahue. He invited Troy to become a Bruin. For Aikman, it was a second chance to become a starter, this time for a team that liked to throw the ball. And it was a chance to go back to Southern California for the first time since he was a young boy.

Aikman felt as if his dreams had all come true. Now he just had to show how talented he could be.

Chapter 3

Top Pick

When Troy arrived on UCLA's campus in 1987, the school already had a starting quarterback. His name was Brendan McCracken. The Bruins' quarterback coach, Rick Neuheisel, expected that Aikman wouldn't know much about passing because his old school, Oklahoma, didn't throw much. The new guy figured to be a backup, nothing more. But when they met, Neuheisel found himself staring at Aikman's big, muscular frame. And when they shook hands, Aikman's hand was so big that it seemed to swallow the coach's. Neuheisel realized then that Troy would be something special.

Actually, Troy had always been special. At UCLA, Troy showed he knew how to throw a speed ball over the middle or a feathery pass just over the defenders' arms. He was always the first one to get to team meetings. He was always the last one out of the weight room because he worked so hard. And he was tough.

At first, Troy's new teammates were not ready to accept him. Many wanted their old buddy, McCracken, to keep the starting job. But Aikman worked hard to win over the other players. And he played so well in practices that everyone, including McCracken, agreed that Troy was the best quarterback on campus.

In his first game, Aikman completed 8 of 10 passes for 166 yards. The Bruins whipped San Diego State, 47–14. A new star had arrived. For the season, Troy went on to complete 65 percent of his passes. He threw for 17 touchdowns and just 8 interceptions. UCLA won 10 of its 12 games, including a victory over Nebraska in the Aloha Bowl.

That great season made Troy a national celebrity. Suddenly, he was regarded as one of the nation's top college football stars. Indeed, before his senior year, many sportswriters predicted Aikman would win the Heisman Trophy.

Some young players might let that kind of attention go to their heads, but not Aikman. He was still a down-to-earth guy. In fact, he spent the summer before his senior year working as a construction worker. No late-night Hollywood parties for Troy. Instead, he worked hard all day, studied his play books at night, and went to bed early.

His hard work and dedication paid off. In 1989, Troy picked up where he left off. He led the Bruins to another 10–2 season and another postseason victory, this time in the Cotton Bowl. As a senior, he passed for 2,771 yards and 24 touchdowns and threw only 9 interceptions. His final statistics made him the third-highest rated passer in collegiate history.

Aikman's final college game was one of his best. On January 2, 1989, he led UCLA on two long touchdown drives to beat Arkansas, 17–3, in the Cotton Bowl. It was a special win for the Bruins because it was their seventh straight bowl victory. That set an NCAA record.

The win didn't come easy. Playing before 74,000 fans, including 150 of his friends and relatives, Troy threw an interception on his third pass. But he quickly recovered and

University of Arkansas linebacker Kerry Owens drags down Aikman. Even in college, Troy was used to physical play. But when he needed to find a way to win, he would do whatever it took to get his team where it needed to be.

led UCLA on scoring drives of 93 and 74 yards. The second touchdown drive was especially impressive. With just two minutes left in the first half, the Bruins got the ball at their own twenty-four-yard line. Troy tried to beat the clock by throwing six straight passes. He completed each one. With just seconds to go in the half, he had a third-and-goal on the Arkansas one-yard line. Troy wrapped the ball under his arm and ran to his right. He was faking a bootleg play. When the Arkansas defenders began to chase him, Aikman flipped a touchdown pass over the line to tight end Corwin Anthony.

After the game, Arkansas safety Steve Atwater was asked his thoughts on Aikman. "He's the $1-million man," said Atwater. "He's very agile and hard to contain on the rollout. He's got great zip on the ball." Atwater said that in his four years of college, Aikman was the best player he had played against.

Was he the best college player in the country? That depends how you look at it. Troy did not win the Heisman Trophy that year. That honor went to Barry Sanders, the Oklahoma State running back. Sanders led all college players in rushing. He, too, would become an NFL Hall-of-Famer.

Most experts, however, agreed that Troy was the college player who would make the biggest splash in pro football. In fact, many people called him the best quarterback prospect since John Elway left college in 1983. When the NFL draft rolled around in April 1989, there was no doubt that the first pick would be the tall, strong kid from Henryetta, Oklahoma.

The NFL draft allows the team with the worst record to pick the best young player. The Dallas Cowboys had been to the playoffs five times in the 1980s. But by 1988 they had the worst record in the league. The Cowboys had not had a Super-Bowl-winning quarterback since Roger Staubach retired ten years earlier. Staubach had been Aikman's favorite player when Troy was young.

"You've got to have a good quarterback," said Cowboys president Tex Schramm. "It is, it has been, and it always will be the name of the game. The quarterback has got to win some football games for you. You can squeeze by here and there, but the quarterback will always be the heart of your club."

The lowly Cowboys liked everything they saw in Aikman. Team vice president Gil Brandt went to scout him and came back praising Troy's size, arm, athletic ability, work habits, character, toughness, and intelligence.

The club dropped a few hints that it would consider trading the top draft pick. No one really believed it. Aikman seemed too perfect a fit for Dallas.

And that was fine with Troy. The Cowboys had been his favorite team since he moved to Oklahoma as a boy. He liked their field at Texas Stadium. He liked their uniforms, with the shiny blue star on the helmet. He liked their coach, Tom Landry.

Make that, he liked Dallas' former coach. On February 25, 1989, Arkansas millionaire Jerry Jones bought the Dallas Cowboys. Jones's first move was to fire Coach Landry and hire a new head coach, Jimmy Johnson. Aikman and Johnson had an interesting history. When Johnson was the head coach at Oklahoma State in 1984, he almost convinced Troy to play there. In 1985, when Troy was at Oklahoma, Johnson became the

The Dallas Cowboys made Aikman the No. 1 overall pick of the 1989 NFL Draft.

head coach at the University of Miami. It was against Johnson's team that Aikman had broken his ankle, which knocked him out for the season. Then, when Troy transferred from Oklahoma, Johnson tried without luck to lure him to Miami.

So this was Johnson's third chance to get Troy. He didn't waste any time. Even before the draft, the Cowboys and Aikman began working on a deal. They got it wrapped up the day before the draft. Aikman received a six-year, $11 million contract. It was the most money ever promised to a first-year player. Aikman was presented with a new No. 8 Cowboys jersey. He then was led to his locker and introduced to his teammates. The next day he flew to New York City to meet NFL Commissioner Pete Rozelle and face reporters.

"I have dreamed about being in this spot all of my life," Aikman told the reporters. "I set some pretty high goals at an early age and I'm not going to let anything stand in my way. When I was growing up, I watched Roger Staubach on TV quite a bit. Every time we turned on the TV, the Cowboys were on. It seems like they never lost a game. They could be down three touchdowns with a minute to play and they'd win. I guess people have had a hard time trying to fill his shoes. I'll try to do my best."

It was modest talk, the kind he had learned from his dad. Ken Aikman had always told his son to lead by actions, not by words. One of Troy's first actions after signing was to establish yearly $5,000 scholarships at Henryetta High and UCLA. He also promised to donate $1,000 to charity for each game won by the Cowboys.

Nice as he was, there were still some questions about how older Cowboys might react to this rookie. Troy's salary made him the club's best-paid player before he had even walked onto an NFL field. It would be natural for some veterans to be jealous. And, just like when Aikman moved to UCLA, there was a popular starting quarterback already in place in Dallas. Steve Pelluer hadn't won many games for the Cowboys, but he had won a lot of friends.

Troy kept quiet and decided to let his arm do the talking. The Cowboys used a special first-round pick that summer to draft Steve Walsh. But Aikman did not complain. He was

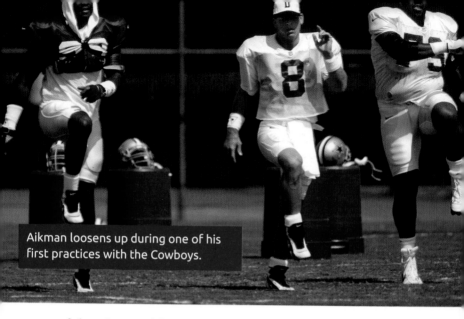

Aikman loosens up during one of his first practices with the Cowboys.

confident he could win the starter's job by working extra hard and showing his talent.

And he did. When the 1989 regular season opened, top draft pick Troy Aikman was the starter. The Cowboys had a new quarterback, a new coach, and twenty new players. The fans in Dallas were excited. It was a new era for the team. Maybe, fans figured, the Cowboys would return to the form that put them in five Super Bowls in the 1970s. Maybe, Aikman would be the man to lead them there.

Troy certainly hoped so. He entered his rookie season full of confidence. Would the Cowboys have a winning record? Would they make the playoffs? Troy believed that they might.

He would soon find out that the NFL was tougher than he had expected.

No Pain, No Gain

Troy Aikman knew that pro football would be tough. He did not expect to come straight from UCLA and dominate the NFL. The pro players were bigger, faster, and more experienced than those he faced in college. His rookie season would be one for learning, he figured.

Troy's first year was twice as tough as he had expected. When a rookie quarterback plays for a losing team, he must quickly learn how to take shots from opposing players. The 1989 Cowboys were a team of inexperienced young players and over-the-hill older players. As a result, Aikman got little blocking and spent much of that year flat on his back, staring up at the opponents who decked him.

Actually, things started out well. The Cowboys opened with four preseason games. Dallas won three of the four games. Aikman looked terrific. In his first preseason game against the San Diego Chargers, Aikman completed 8 of 11 passes. He threw a nine-yard touchdown pass to Kelvin Martin. And he launched a fifty-one-yard bomb to second-year receiver Michael Irvin. After the game, Irvin said he had been wondering if Troy had a strong enough arm to throw such a long pass. Now he knew. "He can throw as deep as I can run," Irvin said. "I think he's going to have a great season."

That's not exactly how things turned out. Once the real season began, opposing teams took things more seriously. The Cowboys had a handful of good players, including Irvin and running back Herschel Walker. But new coach Jimmy Johnson had gotten rid of most of the older players. He replaced them with inexperienced rookies. The new players showed some promise. But they were not ready to face the likes of the Eagles, Giants, Redskins, and 49ers.

Aikman started the first game of his rookie year. Dallas was shut out by the New Orleans Saints. For the season, the Cowboys went 1–15. Troy didn't play in that one win. He broke his index finger against the New York Giants and had to sit out a month. The Cowboys lost all twelve games in which he played. The team's only win came with the other rookie quarterback, Steve Walsh, running the show.

Still, there was reason to feel good about Aikman. Troy was fearless. When he took a beating, he went back into the game instead of back to the bench. He showed poise. He didn't get

During his rookie season, Aikman was forced to miss four games due to injury. Unfortunately for Aikman, he continued to take his lumps throughout his career. In this image, he is forced to the turf during the 1997 season.

rattled when faced with new, confusing situations. And he kept his spirits up and tried to rally his teammates to play better. "We may not get to the Super Bowl this season," Aikman told the others. "But if we stick together, we should get there some day."

One man who shared that opinion was Washington Redskins coach Joe Gibbs. After beating the Cowboys 30–7 early that season, Gibbs met with reporters in the locker room. Everyone expected him to praise his own club, but Gibbs's kindest words went to the losing quarterback. "From what I've seen," Gibbs said. "Aikman is very talented, gifted, and tough. He's going to be very bad for the Redskins and the rest of the teams in this division."

Aikman's best game as a rookie came against the Phoenix Cardinals. It was his first game back after the finger injury. Aikman set the NFL single-game rookie record when he

The highlight of Troy's first season was when he set what was then the rookie record for passing yards in a game.

threw for 379 yards. That mark no longer stands, but Troy will remember the game more for one single play. He threw an 80-yard touchdown pass that showed everything that was right with Aikman and wrong with the Cowboys in 1989.

It came late in the fourth quarter with the Cowboys trailing, 17–13. Troy faded back to pass, scrambling to gain more time. From the corner of his eye, he spotted wide receiver James Dixon streaking for the end zone. Troy heaved the ball as far as he could.

At exactly that moment, Aikman was blasted from behind by Cardinals linebacker Anthony Bell. He did a cartwheel before crashing to the ground. He laid there motionless. Blood flowed from his right ear onto the blue star of his helmet. As team doctors began to examine Troy, several coaches on the sideline feared that he had been killed.

He hadn't. But he did suffer a hit to the head that knocked him out for more than five minutes. Despite that, his pass sailed into Dixon's outstretched hands. The touchdown gave Dallas a 20–17 lead with less than two minutes to play.

When Troy finally came to, he didn't believe he had thrown for a touchdown. Then he noticed the changed numbers on the scoreboard. But seconds later, the Cardinals came back to score and win the game, 24–20. Aikman could hardly believe that either.

Despite flashes of brilliance by the rookie quarterback, the Cowboys still couldn't win. They had such a long way to go.

Afterward, Aikman sat on a stool in front of his locker and spoke of his disappointment. "It has been a long season so far," he said. "I don't know how a rookie is supposed to feel. I'm not going to sit here and tell you I feel like a seasoned veteran and know everything teams are trying to do. Because that's not the truth. But I feel good out there for the most part. And I don't want anyone around me to sense that I'm a rookie. I don't want to be a problem."

Troy was hardly a problem for the Cowboys. When the season ended, he had passed for 1,749 yards. That was a record for Dallas rookies. He was chosen for most all rookie teams. He threw 9 touchdowns, which was good. And he threw 18 interceptions, which was bad. Overall, he showed signs that he could be an excellent NFL quarterback. Coach Johnson said

Aikman had the physical and mental talent to lead the Cowboys through the 1990s.

Now, all Johnson had to do was build a solid team around Troy. Actually, the coach started building even during the 1989 season. He traded star running back Herschel Walker for a package of five players and eight draft picks. In 1990 the Cowboys drafted running back Emmitt Smith. Almost immediately, Smith became a superstar. And Smith's great running forced other teams to stop focusing only on Aikman. Through trades and drafts, Johnson kept adding good, young players. He subtracted one; quarterback Steve Walsh, traded to the Saints for three draft picks.

When Walsh was around Aikman seemed to be always looking over his shoulder, wondering if Walsh would steal his job. Now Aikman knew he was the only quarterback in the Cowboys future. His teammates knew it too.

By the time Troy started his second season, he felt much better. The Cowboys might not get to the Super Bowl, he figured, but they would win their share of games.

They did. Starting with the season opener against the San Diego Chargers, Aikman got the ball with two minutes to go and the Cowboys behind by 4 points. He quickly moved the team 53 yards. A 24-yard touchdown pass to Kelvin Martin brought Dallas the win. It was the first of Aikman's career. Afterward, Troy said he felt as if a giant weight had been lifted from his back. "I don't have to listen to people say I can't win a ball game anymore," he said. "People were questioning the kind of team we were going to have. We worked too hard not to become a good football team."

The Cowboys continued to struggle toward their goal. They won seven games in 1990, six more than the year before. But they lost nine. Emmitt Smith rushed for more than 900 yards and was named the NFL's Offensive Rookie of the Year. Other young players kept getting better. But the Cowboys still made too many mistakes. They had much to learn.

Mostly, they needed to learn to better protect the quarterback. Aikman was sacked 39 times that season. At least twice that often, he was hit hard right after passing the ball. He got decked so often that his nickname around the NFL became "Troy Ache-Man." After every game, it seemed, another part of his body was being X-rayed.

The worst day came in the next-to-last game of the season. The Cowboys record was 7–7 at the time. If they could find a way to beat the tough Philadelphia Eagles, they still had some hope of making the playoffs. On the game's fifth play, Aikman was sacked from behind by Eagles defensive end Clyde Simmons. The 300-pound Simmons drove Aikman's right shoulder into the turf and then rolled over it.

Troy was badly hurt. His shoulder was separated. He was out for the game, which the Cowboys lost, 17–3. And he missed the final game of the season, which they also lost. As soon as the season ended, Troy had two operations. His shoulder was popped back into place. Bone chips were removed from his right elbow. Doctors told him he would be as good as new. They also told him he had been taking too many hits. If he wanted to

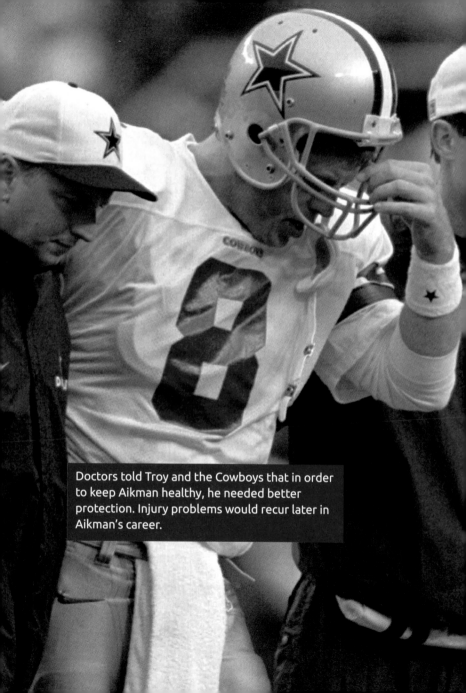

Doctors told Troy and the Cowboys that in order to keep Aikman healthy, he needed better protection. Injury problems would recur later in Aikman's career.

keep playing football, he would have to get better protection from his teammates.

The last message, actually, went straight to Jimmy Johnson. The Cowboys coach listened. In his mind, the team was on the verge of becoming great. All that was needed was a strong offensive line. So Johnson built that line. Through trades, draft picks, and free agent moves, he assembled a crew of giants: center Mark Stepnoski, guards John Gesek and Nate Newton, and tackles Erik Williams and Kevin Gogan. The five men averaged 6 feet, 5 inches and 301 pounds. Their size and strength would keep would-be tacklers away, Johnson figured.

The coach was right. And the Cowboys, led by a well-protected Aikman, would finally become winners.

Chapter 5

Champion

Before the 1991 season, Aikman spent a month back home in Oklahoma. He wanted to escape from the pressures in Dallas. He wanted to clear his head. So he returned to Henryetta, driving a new car he bought as a surprise for his mom. He visited his older sisters, Tammy and Terri. He spent hours playing with his nieces and nephews. He even hung around his old high school pals, playing relaxed games of catch.

In his own way, Troy was preparing for a new season. He wanted to do it his way. He wanted to remember what had made him so successful in high school and college. He wanted to find that formula and bring it to the Cowboys. He was tired of losing.

After a month, Troy found what he was looking for. The

solution seemed too simple. "I've got to start being myself," he told friends. "I've got to stop trying to become the quarterback that others want me to be, and start doing what I do best."

That meant playing in his own style, passing the ball with his special quick release. It meant acting more like himself, instead of what he felt others wanted him to be. It meant having more confidence in his decisions.

Aikman flew back to Dallas and shared his ideas with Coach Jimmy Johnson. Surprisingly, Johnson liked them. Following Troy's ideas, the Cowboys began a quick-release offense, designed to keep the quarterback in one piece. And Johnson told Troy to take more control of the club. "Change the plays at the line of scrimmage if you like," Johnson said. "Become a team leader. It's your third year," the coach told Troy. "It's your time to become a star."

The strategy worked. In 1991, Troy grew from a battered quarterback into a leader. He threw for 2,754 yards and completed 65 percent of his passes. Both were career highs. And he threw just 10 interceptions. Dallas's beefy new offensive line got a lot of the credit. So did Coach Johnson's new offense. Troy's determination and maturity played a big part. His plan to change his ways and play in the style that made him a success in high school and college had worked.

The Cowboys won 11 games in 1991 and lost just 5. They made the playoffs for the first time in six years. They even beat the Chicago Bears in the playoffs before being knocked out by the Detroit Lions. It was a great season for the club.

Sadly, Troy wasn't around for all of it. In the season's twelfth

Head Coach Jimmy Johnson listened to his quarterback and allowed Aikman to have more control of the offense for the 1991 season. Aikman and Johnson maintained a close relationship long after Troy's playing career ended.

game, he was tackled hard by Washington Redskins defensive end Charles Mann. Aikman sprained his knee on the play. He missed the season's last four games and the first playoff game while backup Steve Beuerlein filled in. Troy came back to play in the playoffs against Detroit.

The season ended in a disappointing 38–6 loss to the Lions. Still, there was a lot to be excited about in Dallas. Aikman was picked to play in his first Pro Bowl, the NFL's all-star game. He and his teammates figured that 1991 was a preview of great things to come. Others agreed, including Roger Staubach. The former Cowboys star quarterback had been Troy's hero as a youngster. After watching the 1991 season, Staubach made a bold prediction that the Cowboys would be in the next Super Bowl. And Troy Aikman would lead them there.

Staubach was right. In 1992, Troy and the Cowboys finally put it all together. The team won 13 regular-season games and lost just three. Aikman threw 23 touchdowns. He ranked third in passer rating. Behind a now-solid offensive line, he stayed healthy the entire season. He had emerged as the star everyone predicted he would be.

The Cowboys had many stars in 1992. Running back Emmitt Smith led the NFL with 1,713 rushing yards and 18 touchdowns. Wide receiver Michael Irvin caught 78 passes. In all, six players on the team were chosen for the Pro Bowl.

The key man, though, was Aikman. "When you prepare for the Cowboys, it begins with Aikman," said San Francisco 49ers coach George Seifert.

"It's easy to take him for granted because they're so talented that moving the ball looks easy. But he's big and strong. He's got an accurate arm. And he's got a leadership quality about him."

Seifert was about to find out how super Aikman could be. In January 1993 the 49ers and Cowboys met in the NFC title game. The winner would go to the Super Bowl. The Cowboys had not been to the Super Bowl in fourteen years. Aikman had the chance to be a hero in Dallas.

Aikman accomplished his mission. Against San Francisco, he completed 24 of 34 passes for 322 yards and 2 touchdowns. He led the Cowboys to a 30–20 victory.

His best work was in the second half. Troy directed three touchdown drives to win the game. He was nearly perfect, completing 13 of 16 passes. Mostly, Aikman did what he does best. He didn't turn the ball over. He dented the defense with short passes underneath. When the time was right, he hurt the 49ers with the long pass.

Late in the game, the 49ers scored. The Dallas lead was just 24–20, and the game seemed ready to slip away. Aikman got the ball on his own twenty-four-yard line. Some of the team's coaches wanted to play it safe and try a few running plays, but Aikman convinced head coach Jimmy Johnson to go for it all.

On first down, Troy faked a handoff to Smith. Then he faded back and lofted a perfect pass into the hands of wide receiver Alvin Harper. The San Francisco defenders were surprised. Harper ran seventy yards, all the way to the San Francisco six-yard line. Three plays later, Aikman hit wide receiver Kelvin Martin with a touchdown pass.

The game belonged to Dallas. The Cowboys were going to the Super Bowl.

"I think a lot of people didn't know Troy would be as good as he is," said wide receiver Michael Irvin. "He's a one-of-a-kind guy. He has all the confidence in the world in his ability. We believe in him too."

Irvin and his teammates had reason to believe. After three years of frustration, the guy they called "Ache-Man" had come into his own. Now he needed to have one more big game.

The Cowboys faced the Buffalo Bills in Super Bowl XXVII. While Aikman and nearly all of his young teammates had never been there before, the Bills were back for their third straight appearance. Buffalo had lost the two previous Super Bowls, to the New York Giants and the Washington Redskins. Now the Bills were hungry for a title.

Buffalo was led by quarterback Jim Kelly. Like Aikman, he was a Pro Bowl star. Otherwise, the two men couldn't be more different. Kelly was loud and friendly. He liked to go to parties and to tell jokes. Aikman, as a player, was quiet and a bit of a loner.

The two quarterbacks' playing styles were also different. Kelly was a daredevil. Sometimes he defied the odds by throwing to receivers who seemed to be covered. It caused more interceptions. But it created more touchdowns for his team, too.

Aikman was more careful. He rarely threw the ball into double-coverage. Instead, he stood in the pocket, searching

Aikman offers words of encouragement to losing quarterback Jim Kelly after Super Bowl XXVII. Dallas won the game, 52–17. Although they seemed to have little in common, these two opposing quarterbacks were able to remain friends.

until the last possible moment for an open receiver. The result was that he was often sacked for a loss or nailed by a tackler.

But he threw few interceptions.

Super Bowl XXVII was held on January 31, 1993. It was billed as a battle between the two quarterbacks. Sure, there were other great players on both teams: runners Emmitt Smith of the Cowboys and Thurman Thomas of the Bills; receivers Michael Irvin of the Cowboys and Andre Reed of the Bills. Aikman and Kelly were the players who best represented what their teams stood for. Everyone wanted to see which quarterback would come out on top.

It wasn't even close. The Cowboys rode over the Bills, winning 52–17. Kelly tossed two interceptions and was knocked out of the game in the second quarter. Aikman, meanwhile, was brilliant. After a slow start, he passed for 272 yards and 4 touchdowns.

It all started clicking for Aikman and his speedy band of receivers on their third drive. The Bills had taken a 7–0 lead. The drive started as poorly as Dallas' first two. Emmitt Smith lost a yard on first down. On second down, Aikman's pass to Smith ended up losing another five.

On third-and-sixteen from the Dallas forty-seven, Irvin ran a square-in pattern. The Cowboys offensive line gave Aikman time, and he fired a twenty-yard strike to Irvin that seemed to lift the entire team. Three plays later, Aikman connected with tight end Jay Novacek over the middle of the field for a twenty-three-yard TD.

Once the TDs started coming, they kept coming. Dallas got stronger as the game wore on. In the end, Dallas' 35-point win was the third-highest margin of victory in Super Bowl history.

Aikman was everyone's choice for the game's MVP award. He did a commercial for Disney World while running off the field. In the locker room afterward, he was handed his MVP trophy.

He used the moment to remember his rookie season. The Cowboys went 1–15 that year. Troy had spent much of that season on his back, looking up. As reporters gathered around, Aikman said, "Those were tough days. At times I felt a little overwhelmed. It's hard to believe that in four seasons we've gone from being that bad to being champions. It's a sweet feeling."

The only thing that would make it sweeter would be another Super Bowl title.

Troy (left) chats with former Cleveland Browns quarterback Bernie Kosar and Hall-of-Fame quarterback Dan Marino during the Quarterback challenge in Disney World. This took place about two months after Aikman's Super Bowl XXVIII victory.

The Ultimate Team Player

Every great quarterback has his own style. Just look at the greats of past decades: Baltimore's Johnny Unitas, the best of the 1950s, was cool and calm. Joe Namath, the New York Jets star of the 1960s, was a daredevil. He would brag, and his predictions would come true. He could also flick his wrist and make the football fly seventy yards.

Another Cowboy, Roger Staubach, was the best of the 1970s. "Roger the Dodger" played on guts. He wasn't afraid of banging heads with giant linemen. He did whatever it took to win a game.

The 1980s had many great quarterbacks. Miami's Dan Marino was a precise passer. 49ers legend Joe Montana was a

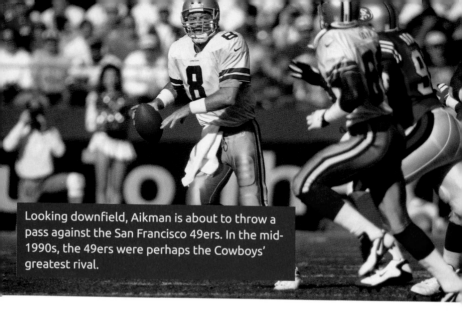

Looking downfield, Aikman is about to throw a pass against the San Francisco 49ers. In the mid-1990s, the 49ers were perhaps the Cowboys' greatest rival.

clutch player who always seemed to steal victories in the end. Philadelphia's Randall Cunningham was a ballet dancer among the NFL brutes.

And then there is Troy Aikman.

"He'll be the quarterback of the 90s," said Staubach at the time. "Troy has got it all."

He sure did. Talk with men who played with Aikman and against him and they'll tell you this: He was strong, accurate, and cool. He was a leader and a winner.

The last word is the key. Some quarterbacks think they need to pass for 350 yards to be a star. Not Troy. He threw for 350 yards only once in his first four years in Dallas, and the Cowboys lost that game. "My goal is for the team to win," Aikman says. "It's not to make myself look good."

Many consider Troy to have been the ultimate team player. No one in football prepared more for each game. No one stayed up later at night, studying the game films. No one listened more closely to his coaches. No one took more pride in victory, even if his teammates emerged as bigger stars.

He was also tougher than most fans thought. Away from football, Aikman had a clean-cut, golly-gee, boy-next-door image. But other Cowboys said he was downright tough, too. If a receiver made a wrong turn on a pass route, Troy would get in his face. If teammates didn't take a practice seriously, Troy would pick up the football and angrily punt it away. "He just wants everything to be right. To be perfect," said former Cowboys guard John Gesek. "It's a matter of pride with him."

It's not surprising that when Aikman was asked after the 1993 season if he saw himself as the Quarterback of the 1990s, he shook his head no. "I've only won one Super Bowl," he said. "I've got a ways to go."

Just days after winning the 1993 championship, Troy set about trying to get back to the Super Bowl. He and the other Dallas players wanted to be a dynasty. That's a team that wins championships year after year. "I don't want to be greedy," Aikman told reporters. "But I'd love to win two of them."

So did Cowboys owner Jerry Jones. Soon after the 1993 season started, Jones signed Aikman to a new contract. It would pay the twenty-seven-year-old quarterback $50 million over the next eight years. The deal made Troy the highest-paid player in NFL history.

Still, the season started badly for Dallas. Running back

Emmitt Smith did not play in the first two games. The Cowboys lost both. Then, toward mid-season, Troy missed two games with a pulled hamstring muscle. The team lost one of those.

But when Aikman and Smith were in the lineup together, the Cowboys were nearly unbeatable, winning 11 of 12 games. Overall, the club went 12–4. Dallas won the NFC East title for the second straight year.

Aikman threw just 6 interceptions in the regular season, the lowest total in team history. He completed 69 percent of his passes, the fourth-best in NFL history. It was an incredible season. And teammates Smith and Michael Irvin chipped in. Together, the three stars combined for 5,916 yards and 31 touchdowns. That easily made Dallas most people's choice to return to the Super Bowl.

To get there, they had to win two playoff games. The Cowboys first faced the Green Bay Packers. The Packers were led by Reggie White, the NFL's best defensive end at the time. Dallas won as Troy completed 75 percent of his passes for more than 300 yards.

Next, the Cowboys faced the San Francisco 49ers. It was a rematch of the previous year's NFC Championship Game.

The game was going great for Dallas. Troy completed 14 of 18 passes and threw touchdowns to Smith and tight end Jay Novacek. By the third quarter, the Cowboys had built a 28–7 lead and the hometown fans were cheering wildly.

Then, a near-disaster struck. San Francisco defensive tackle Dennis Brown accidentally banged Aikman's helmet with his right knee during a sack. Troy rose slowly, holding his helmet with both hands. When he went back to the sidelines, he seemed so confused that team doctor J.R. Zamorano decided to ask him a few questions.

"What day is it?" Zamorano asked Aikman.

"I don't know."

"Who are we playing?" Zamorano said.

"I don't know."

"Where's the Super Bowl?"

"The what?" Aikman replied.

"The Super Bowl, where you were MVP last year."

"I was?"

"Where do you play the next game?"

"Henryetta," said Troy, referring to his hometown.

With that, Aikman was taken to the hospital. The Cowboys held on to win the game. But tests showed that Troy had a concussion. Teammates and fans worried that he might miss the Super Bowl.

Troy was determined that wasn't going to happen. He returned to practice five days later. The Cowboys again faced the Buffalo Bills in the Super Bowl. If they could win, Troy would become the youngest quarterback in NFL history with championship rings on two fingers.

He was not to be denied. Just as they had the year before, the Cowboys stampeded the Bills. Playing before 72,817 fans at the Georgia Dome in Atlanta, Dallas won easily, scoring 30 points to Buffalo's 13.

This time, it was Emmitt Smith's turn to be a star. At the beginning of the second half, with the scored tied, 13–13, Smith carried the ball on 7 of the next 8 plays. He covered 61 yards, ending with a 15-yard touchdown scamper. Smith finished the game with 132 yards and 2 touchdowns on 30 carries. He was named the MVP.

Aikman did his part, too. On the Cowboy's first play of the day, he showed that he wanted a wide-open game. Instead of running (as the Bills had expected) Aikman hit Michael Irvin on a deep slant-in for 20 yards. The play led to a field goal by Eddie Murray.

Late in the first quarter, Aikman found Alvin Harper wide-open on another deep slant route. Aikman hit Harper between the "8" and the "0" on Harper's jersey for a 24-yard gain. That set up another Dallas field goal.

Throughout the game, Troy showed his coolness under pressure. When the Bills fell behind, they began blitzing. Buffalo sent five or six pass rushers at a time. But Troy stood calmly in the pocket. He waited until the last possible instant to throw the ball. Early in the fourth quarter, for instance, the Bills sent everyone after Aikman. He beat them with a 16-yard strike to Harper. That took the ball to Buffalo's six-yard line. Four plays later, Smith made his second touchdown run. Dallas had clinched the game. The Cowboys became the first team since the 1989–90 San Francisco 49ers to win back-to-back Super Bowls.

In the locker-room celebration afterward, Aikman was absolutely gleeful. "It's the greatest feeling in the world," he said. "The second time feels better than the first time. And I can't wait for the third time."

A third time seemed possible. The Cowboys remained one of the NFL's best teams. They still had Aikman, Smith, and Irvin, plus a collection of other stars. But after their second Super Bowl win, the Cowboys went through a big change.

Head Coach Jimmy Johnson quit the team after a public argument with owner Jerry Jones. Johnson was the brains behind the Cowboys. He was the person who put in the system that helped turn the last-place Cowboys into a winning team.

Johnson was replaced by Barry Switzer, the coach at the University of Oklahoma when Troy went there. He is the coach who loved the offense that Troy hated so much.

As an NFL coach, Switzer did not try to change Aikman. He decided to let the Cowboys play as Coach Johnson had played them. It was good news for Troy.

Throughout the 1994 season, the Cowboys and San Francisco 49ers battled it out to see which team was best. Aikman missed two games because of a hand injury. When he came back in a game against the 49ers, he was not sharp. He threw 3 interceptions and the Cowboys lost.

Dallas finished the season with 12 wins and just 4 losses. The Cowboys creamed the Green Bay Packers in the playoffs and then got another chance to face the 49ers in the NFC Championship Game.

This year, however, it was not to be for Dallas. Troy threw 3 interceptions and San Francisco won the game, 38–28. It was a disappointment for the Cowboys. But the loss made Troy and his teammates more dedicated to get back there after the next season.

Troy Aikman and Jimmy Johnson celebrate their Super Bowl XXVIII win. Unfortunately, Johnson would soon quit after a dispute with owner Jerry Jones.

"If I play twelve more years, I want to win twelve more Super Bowls," Aikman said. "Once you make the Super Bowl and win it, then I think you realize the only reason you're playing is to win the Super Bowl."

After the 1994 season, the Cowboys made a huge free agent signing. Dallas brought in the reigning NFL Defensive Player of the Year, Deion "Prime Time" Sanders. With Sanders in the fold, the Cowboys were among the favorites to get back to the Super Bowl.

Aikman and the Cowboys opened the 1995 season with four straight victories. The team appeared to be even better than those that had won the Super Bowl.

In week five, Dallas took on the Washington Redskins, a division rival. After taking a hard hit, Aikman was forced to leave the game. It became the Cowboys first loss. The next week, Troy was back and playing great. He passed for over 300 yards, leading the Cowboys past the Green Bay Packers, 34–24.

Aikman guided the Cowboys to an 8–1 record before the rival 49ers came to town. At the time, the 49ers were struggling. Their record was only 5–4. But the Cowboys got off to an awful start in the game, and never could seem to keep up. After the first quarter, the 49ers were leading 17–0. Aikman was forced to leave the game early once again with an injury after only six pass attempts. He watched from the bench as his Cowboys lost, 38–20.

The Cowboys recovered to win the NFC East, finishing 12–4. Their first playoff game was against the Philadelphia Eagles. The game was not even close. Aikman completed all but seven of his passes. Dallas destroyed the Eagles defense, winning 30–11.

The NFC Championship Game would bring the tough Green Bay Packers. The Cowboys had knocked Green Bay out of the playoffs each of the previous two years. The Packers challenged the Cowboys to a hard-fought game for three quarters. But Green Bay couldn't fight off the Cowboys' tough offensive line and even tougher running back, Emmitt Smith. Smith scored two touchdowns in the fourth quarter to send the Packers home for the third year in a row, 38–27. Aikman finished the game with two touchdown passes and 255 passing yards. He had led Dallas to the big game for the third time in four years.

The Cowboys would face the Pittsburgh Steelers in Super Bowl XXX. Back in the 1970s, the rivalry between the Steelers and Cowboys was perhaps the biggest in the league. The Steelers had beaten the Cowboys in Super Bowl's X and XIII. The Cowboys had also won two Super Bowls in the 1970s but none against Pittsburgh. Restarting this rivalry made the game one of the most anticipated Super Bowls of all time.

The Cowboys started the game off by scoring on their first three drives. Two field goals from kicker Chris Boniol and a three-yard TD pass from Aikman to tight end Jay Novacek, made the score 13–0. But with 13 seconds before halftime, Steelers quarterback Neil O'Donnell threw a six-yard TD pass to Yancey Thigpen.

About halfway through the third quarter, the Steelers were starting to move the ball. They were at midfield when

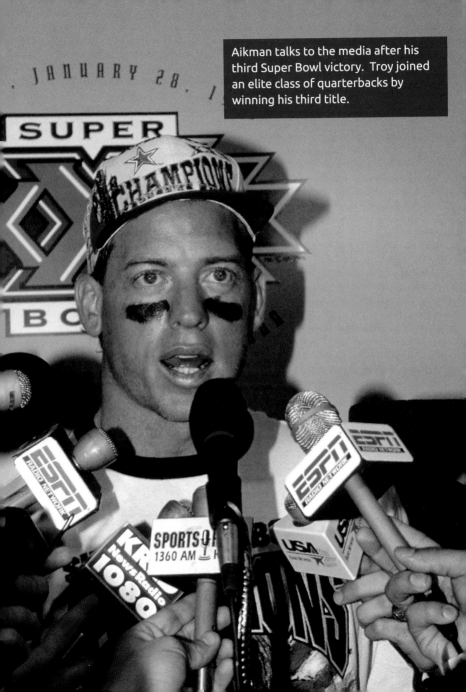

Aikman talks to the media after his third Super Bowl victory. Troy joined an elite class of quarterbacks by winning his third title.

O'Donnell rifled the ball downfield. Unfortunately for the Steelers, O'Donnell threw it right to Cowboys cornerback Larry Brown.

The game was still close in the fourth quarter with 4:15 left. The Cowboys lead was only 20–17. The Steelers made a critical stop and forced the Cowboys to punt. But on the second play of the Steelers drive, Brown was there again to intercept another pass. He ran it back to the Steelers six-yard line. After this, Emmitt Smith came in and bulldozed his way to another score. The game clock ran out, and the Cowboys were champions yet again. Larry Brown was named the game's MVP.

That would be the last Super Bowl win in Aikman's career. Aikman won his final playoff game the following year. It was a wildcard win over the Minnesota Vikings.

From 1997 until 2000, Troy remained quarterback of the Dallas Cowboys. But Dallas struggled as its star players aged. Aikman took a beating in those last years, suffering several concussions.

On April 9, 2001, Troy Aikman officially retired as a Dallas Cowboy. Aikman finished his career as the Cowboys all-time leading passer with 32,942 yards.

Upon retiring as a player in 2001, Aikman remained very active. He joined the Fox network's broadcast team, calling games with Joe Buck and Cris Collinsworth. In 2005, Aikman teamed up with Roger Staubach to form Hall of Fame Racing, a NASCAR racing team. He is partial owner of the Major League Baseball's San Diego Padres. And Aikman also once owned a Ford dealership in Texas.

Troy also loves to try new adventures such as becoming involved in real estate. And he continues his charity work with the Troy Aikman Foundation. In 2010, he became part of the National Football Foundation's Board of Directors. Later that same year, he became a co-spokesman of Rent-A-Center with pro wrestler Hulk Hogan. In 2006, Troy Aikman was inducted into the Pro Football Hall of Fame in Canton, Ohio. He was honored for the amazing career he had. In his induction speech he said:

As I look at the men on this stage behind me, I think about the many great moments that they helped produce. The championships their teams won and the fans they entertained. They all made significant contributions to their teams, and that's why they're here.

In Dallas, my role as the quarterback was to move our team down the field and score points. Sometimes that meant passing the ball; sometimes it meant handing it off. We had a good system in Dallas. Although it wasn't one that allowed me to put up big numbers, that was fine. I did what was asked to help the team win. So it is extremely gratifying that after a career of putting team accomplishments in front of personal achievement, today I am receiving the greatest individual honor a football player could ever receive.

This would be followed by an induction into the College Football Hall of Fame in 2008. His legacy will always live on in Dallas as one of the greatest quarterbacks to ever play.

Aikman poses with his bust after giving his Pro Football Hall of Fame enshrinement speech on August 5, 2006.

Career Statistics

YEAR	CLUB	PASS ATT	PASS COMP	PASS YDS	PCT	TD	INT
1989	Dallas	293	155	1,749	52.9	9	18
1990	Dallas	399	226	2,579	56.6	11	18
1991	Dallas	363	237	2,754	65.3	11	10
1992	Dallas	473	302	3,445	63.8	23	14
1993	Dallas	392	271	3,100	69.1	15	6
1994	Dallas	361	233	2,676	64.5	13	12
1995	Dallas	432	280	3,304	64.8	16	7
1996	Dallas	465	296	3,126	63.7	12	13
1997	Dallas	518	292	3,283	56.4	19	12
1998	Dallas	315	187	2,330	59.4	12	5
1999	Dallas	442	263	2,964	59.5	17	12
2000	Dallas	262	156	1,632	59.5	7	14
TOTAL		4,715	2,898	32,942	61.5	165	141

PASS ATT = Pass Attempts   PASS COMP = Pass Completions   PASS YDS = Passing Yards
PCT = Completion Percentage   TD = Touchdowns   INT = Interceptions

More Info

Contact Troy Aikman:

Troy Aikman
c/o Aikman Enterprises
PO Box 192309
Dallas, TX 75219
USA

http://www.facebook.com/TroyAikman

http://twitter.com/TroyAikman

On the Internet at:

<http://www.nfl.com/player/troyaikman/2499369/careerstats>

<http://www.pro-football-reference.com/players/A/AikmTr00.htm>

<http://www.aikman.com/>

Index